THE 12 DAYS OF MÁS CHRIST

SCRIPTURAL-BASED CELEBRATIONS
OF THE SAVIOR FOR CHRISTMAS

JODI ORGILL BROWN

Author Photo by: Shauna Eskelsen, Eskel Photography

Visit the author at:

Website: www.jodiorgillbrown.com
Instagram: jodiorgillbrown
Facebook: www.facebook.com/jodi.o.brown

Fulfill
Publishing

Read Jodi's bestselling books,

The Sun Still Shines

Rise Above Depression

Book Jodi to speak at your next event at:

www.jodiorgillbrown.com

TABLE OF CONTENTS

For my parents,
Von and Sherri Orgill,
who taught me to love good,
and to love God, from my earliest
days. Their examples set me on
the path that led me to find
the Savior for myself.

PREFACE

The Meaning of Christmas

My language skills are rudimentary, at best, but one thing I do remember from my school days is that the word *más* means *more* in Spanish. While Christmas* is not originally a Spanish word, I like the message of this combination of terms.

Más Christ.
More Christ.

What could happen if we spent the season truly putting **More Christ** in our lives?

Seek More Christ.
Think More Christ.
See More Christ.
Be More Christ.

The repercussions of such a change would be transformative, emotionally, spiritually, socially, and even physically, for individuals, families, and all of society.
Be More Christ.

Becoming more like Christ is the point of Christmas, but also the very point, purpose, and mission of Christ's mortal life. He set the example so that we might become more like Him, that we might be saved and dwell forever with Him!

Be More Christ to Be With Christ.

There is no greater gift He can give than the atonement already wrought to save our souls and allow us access back to our eternal Father.

May we celebrate *The 12 Days of Más Christ* and invite More Christ into our lives!

HOW TO USE THIS BOOK

The 12 Days of Más Christ is organized by days, with one topic per day, including a personal example and a short scriptural exploration. Each day's reading or activity is short enough to finish in under 10 minutes, while the chapter topics are broad enough to generate additional discussion for families or groups.

-- Jodi Orgill Brown

DAY 1: GIVE TO SOMEONE IN NEED

If you want happiness
for an hour—take a nap.
If you want happiness
for a day—go fishing.
If you want happiness
for a month—get married.
If you want happiness
for a year—inherit a fortune.
If you want happiness
for a lifetime—help someone else.

~Chinese proverb

LIFE MOMENT: MEMORABLE HAPPINESS

With only a few exceptions, it is easier for me to recall the experiences of Christmas, more than the gifts themselves. I remember the excitement of rushing into the living room with my siblings, (lined up by age from youngest to oldest), and the heart-pounding giddiness of "the reveal", when we were at-last allowed to view the room filled with colorful packages. My impatience ran high as my dad tinkered with the large video camera, set to record every precious minute. And then, finally, I can replay with great detail, the sheer joy of tearing off the wrapping paper to discover the treasures within each box.

But the memories most poignant in my mind, are those of tip-toeing to the front door of a friend or stranger in need and dropping off large black garbage bags full of presents and groceries. I held my breath, rather than make a noise and be discovered, and the smiles on my parents' faces matched the delight I felt. Both quietly told me that giving was indeed the best tradition of the holiday. No matter the size or number of gifts for our own celebration, helping others became a sacred family ritual.

Those early experiences taught me that even memories of giving create happiness for a lifetime.

SCRIPTURAL EXPLORATION: THE GIVER

The Lord promises that whatever we give to others will be returned unto us in good measure. But the carnal man is an enemy to God (Romans 8:7), and giving doesn't come easily to the natural man. Perhaps that is why the Savior stresses the importance of giving in one of his most straightforward addresses, the Beatitudes, "It is more blessed to give than receive" (Acts 20:35).

The all-knowing Giver knows that giving fulfills

multiple purposes. Here are just a few:

GIVING DEMONSTRATES OBEDIENCE

*Luke 6:30 Give to every man that asketh of thee;
and of him that taketh away thy goods ask
them not again.*

*Psalms 37:4 Withhold not good from them to
whom it is due, when it is in the power of thine
hand to do it.*

God asks of us only that which is for our good. Yet,
our willingness to choose His will demonstrates our
obedience to His commands. Obedience then reflects
our love for God, and for the recipient of our gifts.

With every mortal request for aid comes a two-fold
opportunity to: 1) Assist our fellowmen, and 2)
Establish our obedience to God.

GIVING QUALIFIES US FOR RECEIVING

*Proverbs 11:25 The liberal soul shall be made fat: and
he that watereth shall be watered also himself.*

Blessings of receiving are predicated upon obedience to
the laws and commands of God. When we give, as
instructed by the Lord, we meet the set requirements to

receive. But unlike our limited earthly giving, the all-powerful Lord reciprocates in abundance, with temporal and spiritual gifts.

GOD LOVES CHEERFUL GIVERS

2 Corinthians 9:7 Every man according as he purposeth in his heart, so let him give; not grudgingly, or of necessity: for God loveth a cheerful giver.

Nothing frustrates the Lord more than when we do not acknowledge His hand in our lives. But, God loves a cheerful giver. The Lord simply wants for us to cheerfully and gratefully receive from Him and cheerfully give to others.

GIVING TEACHES US TO TRUST GOD

Malachi 3:10 Bring ye all the tithes into the storehouse, that there may be meat in mine house, and prove me now herewith, saith the Lord of hosts, if I will not open you the windows of heaven, and pour you out a blessing, that there shall not be room enough to receive it.

The two biggest barriers to giving are fear.

1) Fear of Scarcity: Will there be enough left for me?
2) Fear of Rejection: What if they don't want it/me?

The Lord encourages us to test His promise and "prove me herewith...if I will not open you the windows of heaven". When we give, we overcome our natural fears and show God that we trust Him and His plan. We express our faith in God's ability to provide for us and through us. God fulfills His promise of provision when we trust and obey Him.

GIVING ADVANCES GOD'S KINGDOM

When we give, we touch the lives of the receivers. Our gifts may not be the sole source of conversion, but certainly the Lord uses our gifts to touch hearts, reach souls and turn spirits to Him. Whether it be locally or globally, when we give, we invest in the spiritual and eternal welfare of people from every nation, tribe, kindred, tongue and people. Our contributions of money, time and resources transform houses into homes, change relationships, improve countries, and save souls.

GIVING HONORS GOD

Proverbs 3:9 Honour the Lord with thy substance, and with the firstfruits of all thine increase.

Giving promotes God's work, through us and in us. It

purifies our hearts and turns us to the Savior of the world. Our gifts, especially when they come at a sacrifice for us, require that we turn from self to other. In giving up our biological tendencies, we weaken and even break our sinful and selfish natures, and God's grace grows in place of sin. He tells us that our every action to help and strengthen others honors Him. Indeed, all of mankind becomes proxy for the Lord and our actions become proof of our love.

GIVING HELPS US BECOME MORE LIKE CHRIST

2 Corinthian 8:9 For ye know the grace of our Lord Jesus Christ, that, though he was rich, yet for your sakes he became poor, that ye through his poverty might be rich.

God is the source of every good and perfect gift (James 1:17). He is The Giver. As we strive to invite Him into our lives, the truth will grow in our hearts.

James wrote: "If any of you lack wisdom, let him ask of God, that giveth to all men liberally, and upbraideth not; and it shall be given him," James 1:5. God, we learn, is a liberal giver. As we give, and give liberally, we become more like Him.

The Lord gave all for us. Through His poverty we can be made rich. Through our poverty can others be made rich and can we be made rich in Christ.

GIVING BETTER THAN GETTING?

The Lord indeed rewards us — and others — through our giving. He ensures that we receive more than we give. In return for our donations, he bestows gifts and blessings unto us in great abundance. Now, go GIVE!

Luke 6:38 Give, and it shall be given unto you; good measure, pressed down, and shaken together, and running over, shall men give into your bosom. For with the same measure that ye mete withal it shall be measured to you again.

Más Christ.
More Christ.

DAY 2: FORGIVE

LIFE MOMENT: LOSING THE WEIGHT

A few years ago, I spent considerable time with an associate at a conference. We talked intimately and in-depth. She told me that she had run into a couple, staying at the same hotel, whom she had known 30 years before. When they'd last parted ways, she'd been upset by a disagreement. The dispute festered in her and she still carried hurt and anguish from the incident so many years earlier. Like a physical weight, she felt pushed down by her frustrations.

The couple invited her to meet with them that weekend, and she spoke with me prior to the planned gathering. During our visit, she stewed over the possible outcomes with the couple. She harbored much resentment; she could hardly imagine any possibility other than another blow-up fight.

For twenty minutes, I listened to her fears and frets. Then I finally commented, "Wouldn't it be better to let things go, rather than worry about who said what 30 years ago? When I choose to forgive someone, it is for me, more than for them. It makes me free of the hurt and frustration."

I found it quite easy to make the declaration that *she* should forgive. She went to the reunion and reported back to me the following day.

"They embraced me as old friends, said it was wonderful to see me, and they recalled all the fun memories we'd shared together years earlier."

And then the tears began to trickle from her eyes.

"I've fostered so much hate toward them, but they held none of that. When I finally let down my guard and welcomed them back into my life, it was as if I dropped a hundred-pound sack of rocks from my back. I smiled, laughed, and visited with them, in a way I never could have thought possible," she said.

"All that time, I could have chosen to remember the good memories, as they did. Instead, by not forgiving them, I burdened myself."

BEGGING FOR PARDON

The ease of forgiving, which I so eagerly encouraged for my friend, proved harder in my own life, most especially when I was the one who needed to seek forgiveness. In light of my right to express my opinion, I spoke words that hurt a loved one. My actions ate away at me, for I knew I'd endangered a relationship I valued beyond measure.

The scene replayed in my mind over and over again, and heaviness settled in, a similar weight to that carried by my associate for more than 30 years.

No matter how many times I tried to convince my-self *not* to think about it, the thoughts took over my mind.

After tears of sorrow and prayers for strength, I approached my loved one, and begged her pardon. She willingly offered her love and immediately forgave the offense.

But the wrongdoing lingered in my mind, and another realization hit me. I needed to choose to forgive—to Forgive Myself.

SCRIPTURAL EXPLORATION: FOR GIVENESS

Philippians 4:19 But my God shall supply all your need according to his riches in glory by Christ Jesus.

When my youngest son was eight years old, he came home from Sunday School with a paper listing the steps of repentance. Instead of writing on the list *forgiveness*, he wrote 'For Giveness'. This little change created a big change of meaning to me. When we apologize, we are asking for the offended individual to *give* us a restoration of the relationship, trust, and blessings that we lost. We are also asking for God's grace, and his suppliance of our needs.

When we humble ourselves enough apologize and right our wrongs, we allow the atonement of Christ to work in our hearts and spirits.

For the Lord to grant us with the spiritual and temporal blessings we want and need, we must abandon our pride and kneel, not only before our Maker, but before him whom we have offended. Only then can Christ restore all that we lost through our sins.

Matt 11:25 And when you stand praying,
if you hold anything against anyone, forgive them,
so that your Father in heaven may forgive you your sins.

Más Christ.

More Christ.

DAY 3: STRENGTHEN ANOTHER

On a cold bench, a young man sat and thought;
As shoppers loaded cars with presents bought.
With lists checked off, their faces shone,
Yet, still, the boy, he sat alone.
They did not seem to see him there,
Though, one or two did stop and stare.
He had not a flame or spark to even keep going,
Others moved faster, while he was just slowing.
"Is anybody out there, or is it only just me?"
His mind did wonder if it could be.
Then with a wave and a shout of his name,
A schoolmate lifted him out of his shame.
For with one quick hello and a hand in the air,
The solitary boy turned away from despair.
"I am not all alone, there is someone who sees,"
And that, my friends, is how God answers our pleas.

LIFE MOMENT: EARTHLY ANGELS

We've all been there; that place where none of us likes to be. Down in the dumps. At the bottom of the barrel. Fallen off the horse. A few rungs from the bottom of the ladder. Curled up in a ball on the couch. Under the covers in bed. Hiding from the world.

At times, the Christmas season isn't merry and bright, it is a reminder of hard times past, present struggles, and unknown futures.

For a few years, I noticed that every November, my friend's countenance dropped like pine needles after Christmas. When I inquired, he confided that ever since a painful divorce, the season of light was a blackout in his life. The holidays had turned into long, dark months of going through the motions. He wanted nothing to do with Christmas and he dreaded the approach of the season.

Only a few months later, I saw my friend again. This time, he ran to me, smiled, and told me how a co-worker put a little Christmas magic back in his life, simply by including him in holiday and gift-giving activities. Just being remembered and included restored his spirit, and his faith in others. It didn't take away the pain of the divorce, but it affirmed that he was *still* worthy of happiness and joy.

SCRIPTURAL EXPLORATION: LIFT LIVES

When we lift another, we fulfill the law of Christ (Galatians 6:2), enable Him to bless others, and bring the blessing of heaven into our own lives.

The Lord promised to wipe away every tear from our eyes (Revelation 21:4) and to heal the brokenhearted (Psalm 127:3). To fulfill these promises, God needs willing hearts and hands to help do His work.

Letting someone know that THEY MATTER TO YOU is one of the most lasting gifts we can give.

Matt 25: 40 And the King shall answer and say unto them, Verily I say unto you, Inasmuch as ye have done it unto one of the least of these my brethren, ye have done it unto me.

Romans 12:15 Rejoice with them that do rejoice, and weep with them that weep.

Isaiah 40:29 He giveth power to the faint; and to them that have no might he increaseth strength.

Más Christ.

More Christ.

DAY 4: FULFILL AN OBLIGATION

"A promise made is a debt unpaid."
— Robert W. Service

LIFE MOMENT: THE NEED FOR TRUST

In times past, a man's word represented a personal commitment, indeed a vow of his honor. Today, people give their word, sign their consent, and swear a promise, yet still neglect from fulfilling their responsibilities.

Not only does the world need love, sweet love, we also need trust. According to Stephen M.R. Covey, author of *The Speed of Trust*, the fastest way to build trust is to repeatedly fulfill your obligations.

When you think of un-kept obligations—the $25 you owe the neighbor, the raking you promised to do for Dad, or the power bill you still haven't paid—feelings of guilt register in the mind and trigger a reaction in the limbic system. This is the short-term fight-or-flight system that powers you with the emotions to survive. But the thought of little duties left undone can actually start the brain into a *fight* stance and cause the body to launch into defense mode, which further increases anxiety, stress and roller coaster emotions.

So, do yourself a favor and cross an obligation off your "I Owe You" list. It will elevate you in the eyes of the recipient, increase trust, relieve you from guilt and stress, and allow you to think rationally again.

SCRIPTURAL EXPLORATION: STEP CLOSER

Any time we go back on our word, or fail to do what we said we would do, we step away from God.

Perhaps the little pinprick thoughts in the back of the mind are reminders from the Lord to 'just do it'. When we do what we say we are going to do, it aligns our values with our actions—and draws us closer to God.

Leviticus 19:13 Thou shalt not defraud thy neighbour, neither rob him: the wages of him that is hired shall not abide with thee all night until the morning.

Romans 13:7 Render therefore to all their dues: tribute to whom tribute is due; custom to whom custom; fear to whom fear; honour to whom honour.

Más Christ.

More Christ.

DAY 5: GIVE AWAY EXCESS

"The more you give, the less you need."
— *Stephen Richards*

LIFE MOMENT: ENOUGH IS ENOUGH

Many throughout the world do not *need* anything for Christmas. Homes are so full, families rent storage units to hold more stuff. More than ever before in history, a large portion of the population does not face the struggle of *not enough*.

Slim the excess, and free your life from the chaos of maintaining and storing extra possessions. There will be less to clean, less to store, less to worry about, less poverty—and more good will, more happy hearts, and more goodness.

SCRIPTURAL EXPLORATION: GET GIVING

The Lord counseled us not to worry about 'what ye shall put on' (Luke 12:22), nor to hoard earthly treasures that will not last (Matt 13:44). But technology and invention have so eased life that we spend numerous hours and millions of dollars doing just that.

Despite the abundance of *stuff*, the gulf between rich and poor is widening. One of the ways the Lord blesses others is through our giving, so get giving, and get rid of the stress and worry of stuff.

Matt 10:8 Freely you received, freely give.
2 Chronicles 31:10... for the LORD has blessed His people, and this great quantity is left over.

Luke 12:15 Then He said to them, "Beware, and be on your guard against every form of greed; for not even when one has an abundance does his life consist of his possessions."

Deuteronomy 15:7-8 If there is a poor man with you, one of your brothers, in any of your towns in your land which the LORD your God is giving you, you shall not harden your heart, nor close your hand from your poor brother; but you shall freely open your hand to him, and shall generously lend him sufficient for his need in whatever he lacks.

Más Christ.

More Christ.

Day 6: Say a Kind Word

Life Moment: Speak Love

Words are more powerful than swords for transforming lives. Words propel while swords compel.

Indeed, what comes forth from our mouths exceeds in importance to what goes in our mouths.

Compliments and kind words can lift a spirit, brighten a day, or help one feel better, feel loved, feel cared for, or simply keep going. A thoughtful word, a sincere compliment, or even a poignant wish can make all the difference. Take notice of the little things and take time to share. When we give a loving word, we speak not only of the other, but we speak volumes about ourselves.

Scriptural Exploration: Save A Soul

Jesus Christ changed lives and saved souls with His words. In John 8:7, the Savior told the accusers (of the woman taken in adultery) that those without sin should cast the first stones. Those few phrases turned the woman's heart from sin to repentance, and her accusers from scorners into censured souls.

The apostle Paul taught that when we receive gifts of God, we must speak them (1 Corinthians 1:12-13). When we utter those gifts, we share the spirit and light from the Holy Ghost with our fellow men.

Kind words live in the heart and grow infinitely larger when they take root. Like light, once kindness is expressed, it spreads and there is no end to its reach.

Let the light of Christ shine through you to touch a soul—speak a kind word.

Proverbs 16:24 Pleasant words are as an honeycomb, sweet to the soul, and health to the bones.

Job 4:4 Thy words have upholden him that was falling, and thou hast strengthened the feeble knees. Proverbs 31:26 She openeth her mouth with wisdom; and in her tongue is the law of kindness.

Más Christ.

More Christ.

Day 7: Study the Characters

"The Almighty appeared on earth as a helpless human baby, needing to be fed and changed and taught to talk like any other child. The more you think about it, the more staggering it gets. Nothing in fiction is so fantastic as this truth." — J.I. Packer

Life Moment: Picture the Scene

Mary, the Mother of Jesus

Imagine what it must have been like for Mary when she first looked into the stable and saw her *room* for the night. Unlike the clean tidy straw and the perfect cradle-shaped mangers we have in our modern-day nativities, the stable Mary entered featured unclean animals, flies, their accompanying smells and sounds. Yet, perhaps she knew when she viewed that spot for the first time, that it would be a place of something holy and miraculous, despite its current imperfections.

Surely Mary would have preferred the warmth and comfort of a room in the inn, but being an obedient, faithful daughter of God, she accepted the opportunity of motherhood and took her place in the stable.

SCRIPTURAL EXPLORATION: MARY

In order for her child, the literal Son of God, to descend beneath all of mankind, so, too, did Mary, as she laid down amongst the animals for the sacred birth (Luke 2:6-7). But being receptive to her calling, Mary did not see her condition as a trial, but as a blessing. The holy babe allowed her to become a mother and to serve the Lord. As a faithful, righteous handmaid (Luke 1:38), these would have been desires of her heart.

Religious scholar, Susan E. Black, said that from the scriptures we learn, Mary's son, Jesus, inherited "the physical, mental, and spiritual traits of his parents — one, the glorified God; the other, a worthy, blessed mortal woman." Could Mary have had such blessings without experiencing the trials in her life?

The meek young woman freely sacrificed her own will to embrace her role in giving birth to the God of the world. As the chosen vessel of the Savior, her life would be endangered, her family would be hunted, and her son would be sacrificed, yet she magnified and rejoiced in her God and Savior.

"My soul doth magnify the Lord, and my spirit hath rejoiced in God my Savior. For He hath regarded the low estate of His handmaiden," (Luke 1:46-48). Therein lies the beauty of Christmas.

The lowliness of earth. The holiness of God. And the joy we experience when we learn that He is mindful of us.

Luke 1:30 And the angel said unto her, Fear not, Mary: for thou hast found favour with God.

Luke 1:38 And Mary said, Behold the handmaid of the Lord; be it unto me according to thy word. And the angel departed from her.

LIFE MOMENT: TOUGH AND TENDER

JOSEPH, THE HUSBAND OF MARY

Today, men the media portrays men as bumbling fools, sidekicks to their always-right, strong female counter parts. Sometimes they appear solely for comic relief, so it is with great admiration and respect that we look at the role of Joseph as an example of how to be a righteous man. His every action demonstrated his love and commitment to Mary, to marriage, to parenthood, and to the Lord.

SCRIPTURAL EXPLORATION: A VALIANT MAN

A good, honorable man is cherished and respected by those around him (1 Samuel 9:6). Joseph must have been more than simply good or honorable; he must have been valiant in order to qualify to be the husband of the chosen mother, and the earthly father to the eternal king.

Though little is known about Joseph, those actions and deeds we are familiar with were in accordance with the will of the Lord. From his genealogy, given in Matthew 1, we know that Joseph is a direct descendant of David, which is a fulfillment of prophecies noting that Christ would be born through the Davidic line. He was a well-respected man who kept the Judaic laws. Translation of the word *dikaois* (Greek) from Matthew 1:19 suggests Joseph was just and righteous, most especially in the eyes of God, and was elect amongst the Jews.

When he discovered Mary, his betrothed, was with child, his immediate reaction was to keep her from public scorn, to shelter her from the abuse she would surely receive from the world because of her condition. His initial plan to "divorce her [break off the engagement/release her] quietly" was in the best interest of the young woman whose virtue he cared so much about, despite the personal disappointment and frustration he must have been feeling. Though he could have publicly and rightly broken off their engagement and even had her stoned to death because of supposed unfaithfulness, he acted instead out of love, devotion and kindness to Mary.

He took Mary to wife and kept her untouched by the world while she carried the Son of God. They obediently named him Jesus, and Joseph raised the surrogate child as his own son.

From Luke 2:39-40, we know that Mary and Joseph "had performed all things according to the law of the Lord" before returning to Nazareth. Joseph is a mighty example of righteousness, following God's laws and *performing* all things required by the law. He did not just believe, he *acted* in accordance with his faith and knowledge.

We also know from the book of Luke (2:41) that Joseph was devout in his faith and participated in the religious customs of the Jews that time, including the observance of the Passover. He led his family in this religious ceremony and served as an example for how to be a righteous patriarch.

When Jesus tarried at the temple, following the feast of the Passover, his parents sought him, afraid for his welfare. Joseph and Mary did not immediately understand the reason Jesus gave for staying behind, yet their actions demonstrated parental care and concern for their son. When Jesus heard of that concern, he returned home with them, demonstrating His own respect and love for His father and mother.

When God the Father chose a mortal man to raise His own son, Joseph was the chosen man. If you were unable to raise your child, to whom would you give the responsibility? This trust given to Joseph is indicative of the man God knew him to be: a faithful, virtuous, humble, honorable, devoted man of integrity who acted with love and kindness in all things.

We owe much to this humble man who willingly accepted his earthly role as father to the Heavenly King!

Matt 1:24-25 And Joseph awoke from his sleep and did as the angel of the Lord commanded him, and embraced Mary as his wife.

Más Christ.

More Christ.

Day 8: Give Gifts to Christ

Life Moment: Gifts for the King

During the month of December, keep track of ways in which you offer gifts to God. Write in a notebook, journal, or in a present you keep under the tree. Let the record stand as a witness of your faith and love.

Scriptural Exploration: Gift to God

OBEDIENCE

> *Exodus 19:5 Now therefore, if ye will obey my voice indeed, and keep my covenant, then ye shall be a peculiar treasure unto me above all people: for all the earth is mine*

> *Genesis 27:8 Now therefore, my son, obey my voice according to that which I command thee.*

The simplest of all the commandments of God is to obey! When we do as the Lord asks of us, He knows our hearts are pure and He knows He can trust us. Our obedience earns us treasures and blessings, but more importantly, our actions show that, in our hearts, we stand with Him.

OUR WILL

*Luke 22:42 Saying, Father, if thou be willing, remove
this cup from me: nevertheless not my will,
but thine, be done.*

Even Christ, the very Son of God, gave up His will
to complete the holy and divine mission as given by
the Father. Likewise, when we give Him our will,
and give up our own plans for ourselves, we
demonstrate our faith and trust in Him. Our
willingness to depart from our limited thinking and
act in accordance with His will is perhaps the most
powerful gift we can give our Savior. For He *needs*
nothing from us, but desires only to bless us, which
thing He cannot justly do unless our actions fulfill
His predicated laws and commands.

HEART, SOUL, MIND, AND STRENGTH

*Mark 12:30 And thou shalt love the Lord thy God
with all thy heart, and with all thy soul,
and with all thy mind, and with all thy strength:
this is the first commandment.*

The love He asks for requires our dedication, spirit,
thoughtfulness, intelligence and all the energy we
can muster. Using these strong emotions and powers,
we are to oblige the Lord by following Him, serving

our families and fellow men, and doing in all things, as He did. Thus, we show our love by our actions.

TESTIMONY

2 Timothy 1:8 Be not thou therefore ashamed of the testimony of our Lord, nor of me his prisoner: but be thou partaker of the afflictions of the gospel according to the power of God;

2 Corinthians 1:12 For our rejoicing is this, the testimony of our conscience, that in simplicity and godly sincerity, not with fleshly wisdom, but by the grace of God, we have had our conversation in the world, and more abundantly to you-ward.

In the days of Christ, the number of men who received a true testimony of the Savior was miniscule, in comparison to the population of the world. The same is true today. This is the reason our testimonies are needed now, more than ever.

The day of His return draws ever nearer, and it is our responsibility, as hearers of the word, to share the good news of the gospel with our fellow men. We are to open our mouths to proclaim that Christ is the Lord, to let all men, everywhere partake of His goodness and mercy. Give Him of your testimony by sharing it with others.

OUR LIGHT

*John 8:12 Then spake Jesus again unto them,
saying, I am the light of the world: he that
followeth me shall not walk in darkness,
but shall have the light of life.*

*Luke 11:33 No man, when he hath lighted a candle,
putteth it in a secret place, neither under a bushel,
but on a candlestick, that they which come in
may see the light.*

*Matt 5:16 Let your light so shine before men,
that they may see your good works,
and glorify your Father which is in heaven.*

ALL OUR GIFTS

*Numbers 18:29 Out of all your gifts ye shall offer
every heave offering of the LORD, of all the best
thereof, even the hallowed part thereof out of it.*

*Matt 2:11 And when they were come into the house,
they saw the young child with Mary his mother,
and fell down, and worshipped him: and when they
had opened their treasures, they presented unto him
gifts; gold, and frankincense, and myrrh.*

Más Christ.

More Christ.

DAY 9: PRAISE HIM WITH A CHRISTMAS HYMN

LIFE MOMENT: SONGS FOR THE KING

Hymns, by definition, are praises of God which originate from religious poems or scriptures. Their singular purpose is to worship the Lord. Hymns and reverential carols help us feel the Spirit and celebrate Christ.

In 1847, Placide Cappeau de Roquemaure, (1808-1877), a wine merchant and poet, was asked by a local French priest to write a poem to be read at Christmas mass. Cappeau, known for his fine writing, was honored to share his talents with the church, though he was not a Christian. Using the gospel of Luke as his background and guide, he imagined witnessing the Savior's birth in Bethlehem, and penned the beautiful lyrics to "O Holy Night". Moved by his own words, he decided the lines and phrases were more than a poem; they deserved musical accompaniment. He approached Adolphe Charles Adams, (1803-1856), a theatre and opera composer, to write the music. Most known today for the ballet, *Giselle*, Adolphe had attended the Paris conservatoire and forged a career as a musician. His work was to create an original score for Cappeau's words. Just three weeks after completion, the song was performed at Midnight Mass on Christmas Eve. His notes became the tune we know so well.

In 1855, John Sullivan Dwight, (1812-1893), an ardent abolitionist, translated the hymn into English after he was particularly moved by the words of the third verse.

Truly He taught us to love one another;
His law is love and his gospel is peace.
Chains shall He break, for the slave is our brother;
and in his name, all oppression shall cease.

Some of the most beautiful words celebrating Christ came from an unbeliever—a perfect demonstration that the divinity of the Lord triumphs over all.

O Holy Night! The stars are brightly shining,
It is the night of the dear Saviour's birth.
Long lay the world in sin and error pining.
Till He appeared and the Spirit felt its worth.

A thrill of hope, the weary world rejoices,
For yonder breaks a new and glorious morn.
Fall on your knees! Oh, hear the angel voices!
O night divine, the night when Christ was born;
O night, O Holy Night , O night divine!
O night, O Holy Night , O night divine!

May we fall to our knees to praise Him and in so doing, remember and keep Him ever in our lives.

SCRIPTURAL EXPLORATION: SING PRAISES

Psalm 149:5 Let the saints be joyful in glory:
let them sing aloud upon their beds.

Ephesians 5:19 Speaking to yourselves in psalms
and hymns and spiritual songs, singing and making
melody in your heart to the Lord;

2 Samuel 22:50 Therefore I will give thanks unto thee,
O LORD, among the heathen, and I will sing
praises unto thy name.

Más Christ.

More Christ.

DAY 10: CELEBRATE TRADITIONS

"I believe in traditions; I believe in the idea of things being passed between generations and the slow transmission of cultural values through tradition." -- Graham Moore

SCRIPTURAL EXPLORATION: SING PRAISES

The Lord commanded His people to institute ceremonies and religious celebrations to remember important events, as seen with The Passover, (Exodus 12:14). What better way to remember the Savior at Christmas than to participate in beloved traditions, and create new traditions as a covenant to remember the Lord, as he remembers His covenants with us.

LIFE MOMENT: PICTURE CHRISTMAS

Imagine the scene from the first Christmas Day. With great love and rejoicing, mortal parents welcomed the newborn Son of God. All of heaven sang out in song, and even the lowly animals on earth seemed to feel the magnitude of that great day. From re-enacting the nativity to reading the story of His birth, there are countless traditions to celebrate the birth and life of the Savior.

GIFT BOX

Keep a *Gift for Jesus* always under the tree. Fill it with something different each year, a record of testimonies, service done for others, or personal promises to the Savior. Open and present the gift to Christ on Christmas Eve as you celebrate His birth into the world. Perhaps part of your present is the gift box itself. Find representations of the Savior and create a box to hold depictions of your love for the Lord or make a Christ collage to hang in your home.

NATIVITIES

Nativities, whether decorations or live re-enactments, are beautiful reminders of Christ's birth. With each new depiction, choose a different character from the birth story and imagine the scene from their perspective. Look for representations on ornaments, models, figurines, illustrations, paintings and artwork. Explore the event from different cultures and parts of the world.

MANGERS

Display a manger in your home and place a piece of straw within for every Christ-like action. Teach your family that service to the Lord makes a difference. This activity is especially meaningful for young children, as they can see their daily pieces of straw, serving to create a resting place for the Christ child.

SPIRITUALIZE SECULAR TRADITIONS

Add spiritual meaning to secular holiday traditions to make all celebrations about Christ. When you hang stockings on Christmas Eve, include expressions of gratitude for the good, and the God, in life. Turn Santa customs into examples of helping others and good prevailing during the season. Use advent calendars to celebrate scripture by reading about the Savior each day.

GET CREATIVE

Write your own Christmas song or hymn, read daily passages from the Bible, play chimes, draw pictures, make stars or ornaments for your tree; what matters is not the activity itself, but the meaning and the tradition of worshipping the Lord.

Lev 26:42 Then will I remember my covenant with Jacob, and also my covenant with Isaac, and also my covenant with Abraham will I remember; and I will remember the land.

Más Christ.

More Christ.

DAY 11: LOOK UP

LIFE MOMENT: GAZE HEAVENWARD

The shepherds and wise men of old would have missed the signs of the dear Savior's birth had they been looking down. During the night after an otherwise ordinary day, a heavenly symbol and guide shone bright in the sky, but only for those who looked. Much like today, those who close their eyes won't see the miracles. To see the beauties of the world, to see the wonders of heaven, to witness the blessings of God, we must look up!

Today social media would have us stare at photos of friends rather than look them in the face. It is a time when people pass with eyes averted, pretending not to see each other. Rather than welcome others into our lives, we are taught to fear strangers, to trust no one, to lock our doors and shut our gates. The words of the musical, based on Victor Hugo's classic, *Les Miserables*, perfectly state, "Look down, look down. Don't look them in the eye. Look down. Look down. You're here until you die." Satan, the devil and deceiver, would have us look down.

The unchanging and everlasting God would have us look up—unto the heavens, to the mountaintops, and to the sun and stars above, so we may place our focus where He is, and where we can be.

Hold your head high, for you are a child of God! Meet the eyes of strangers, smile as you pass and let Christ's light shine through you that you may praise the Lord with your gaze.

SCRIPTURAL EXPLORATION: SEE

Job 35:5 Look unto the heavens, and see; and behold the clouds which are higher than thou.

Matt 2:9 When they had heard the king, they departed; and, lo, the star, which they saw in the east, went before them, till it came and stood over where the young child was.

Más Christ.

More Christ.

DAY 12: REMEMBER THE MESSAGES OF CHRIST

LIFE MOMENT: THE MESSENGER

Long ago, I learned that when I need direction, *the messages will come,* but the source is as important as the message. For a directive to cause personal action, one must believe the message and trust the messenger.

SCRIPTURAL EXPLORATION: THE MESSAGES

LOVE

Love is THE message of Christ. It was Christ's message to us and it is a gift we can give each other, in His honor. If we truly understand love, we will see that it encompasses all else. If we love Him, we will want to become like Him, and we will love our fellow men in the process, because we will see Him in them.

> *John 13:34 A new commandment I give unto you,*
> *That ye love one another; as I have loved you,*
> *that ye also love one another.*

HIS GIFTS TO US

The true gifts of Christmas are gifts He gave to us: His birth, His life, His mission, His teachings, His atonement, His death, and His resurrection.

The Savior also blessed each of us with specific gifts that help and strengthen us, and those we encounter. His gifts to us are varied and numerous:

- A loving heart
- An eye that sees the needs of others
- Strength to fight the good fight
- A healing touch
- Miracles
- A faithful spirit
- Knowledge
- The ability to find happiness in any situation
- Revelations/Visions
- A mind that discerns truth
- Wisdom
- The love to be a good friend
- Benevolence
- A strong testimony
- Languages
- Empathy
- The ability to easily forgive
- Communication
- The ability to touch others with His spirit
- Endurance

This small list represents only a few of the gifts of the Spirit that God has bestowed upon His children. A more grateful expression of thanks would be to explore and discover the gifts within each of us, so we can more fully use these blessings.

1 Corinthians 12:4 Now there are diversities of gifts, but the same Spirit.

HOPE

Hope is that little spark inside your heart that dares you to believe there is more, more to life, more to live, more to wish for, more to enjoy, more to believe and more to come. It is our hope in Jesus Christ that builds our testimonies and lightens our burdens. We can Hope for all things.

1 Corinthians 13:7 Beareth all things, believeth all things, hopeth all things, endureth all things.

JOY TO THE WORLD

Joy is much more than temporary happiness, it is a feeling that penetrates the soul and fills us, so nothing more is needed. Material possessions may offer fleeting excitement, but they do not bring lasting joy.

Joy comes from knowing the truth, living the gospel and testifying of Christ!

1 Corinthians 13: 6 ... Rejoiceth in the truth

Matt 25:23 His lord said unto him, Well done, good and faithful servant; thou hast been faithful over a few things, I will make thee ruler over many things: enter thou into the joy of thy lord.

CHARITY

Charity is the pure love of Christ. The pure love of Christ is unconditional and all encompassing. Charity does not see color, race, status, background or language; real charity sees only the PERSON in need of love and compassion. We can choose to see each other as real people, and not just as a bad driver, a mean lady, a punk kid, a crusty old man, a rude sales clerk, a demanding customer, a stuck-up snob, or a homeless drunk. Once we decide to see all people as sons and daughters of God, with divine potential, only then can we begin to understand the pure love of Christ.

The power of the pure love of Christ defies description. When we extend charity, God's hands reach down from heaven to bless lives. By extending the Savior's love to all, we indeed can be His hands here on earth.

*1 Corinthians 13:4 Charity suffereth long,
and is kind; charity envieth not; charity vaunteth
not itself, is not puffed up*

1 Corinthians 13:7 Charity never faileth

REMEMBRANCE

Boundless and numberless are the possibilities for honoring the Savior and bringing Him into your home at Christmas. What is important is not the method or activity, but remembering to let Christ into your life.

*Deuteronomy 8:18 Thou shalt remember
the LORD thy God.*

*1 Corinthians 11:2 Now I praise you, brethren, that ye
remember me in all things, and keep the ordinances,
as I delivered them to you.*

*John 14:23 Jesus answered and said unto him,
If a man love me, he will keep my words:
and my Father will love him, and we will come unto him,
and make our abode with him.*

Más Christ.

More Christ.

For every gift you give and
receive, may Christ the Lord,
be at the center of all.

Merry Christmas.

ABOUT THE AUTHOR

Jodi Orgill Brown is the award-winning author of the bestseller, *The Sun Still Shines*, a memoir of her fight for life with a brain tumor, and the Amazon bestselling book, *Rise Above Depression*. She lives in Utah with her husband, and their four children. Jodi is inspired by people who live fulfilled lives in spite of their struggles.

Jodi earned a master's degree in organizational communication from the University of Utah, a bachelor's degree from Brigham Young University, and is a Certified Fund Raising Executive (CFRE), and nonprofit consultant.

CONNECT WITH JODI

www.authorjodibrown.com
Email: authorjodibrown@gmail.com

Facebook: www.facebook.com/jodiobrown
Instagram: jodiorgillbrown

To book Jodi as a keynote speaker, consultant or presenter, contact: ampliodevelopment@gmail.com. Purchase Jodi's books, *The Sun Still Shines*, or *Rise Above Depression*, at Amazon.com or other online book retailers.

Please Leave a Review

If you enjoyed this book or found it useful, please post a short review on Amazon or Goodreads. Your support really does make a difference. The author reads all reviews and appreciates constructive feedback.

Thank you for your support!